DAVID FIKAYOMI OLABODE

Foreword By Terri Savelle Foy

MY VICTORY OVER CANCER

AN EIGHT-YEAR-OLD BOY'S JOURNEY OF FAITH

DEDICATION

This book is dedicated to God Almighty. Without You, I will not be here. You healed me when it looked like there was no hope. You turned my life around. You changed me from a grumpy boy to a God-loving boy full of faith.

ACKNOWLEDGEMENTS

My healing and the testimonies from my journey are probably the best things that have come out of having cancer. That is why I wrote this book.

First, I want to thank the Almighty God for giving me the words to put in this book.

I especially have to thank my mom, Olugbemisola Olabode, for pushing me to write this book. There is one other person who challenged me to write this book, Mrs. Terri Savelle Foy. I started listening to her a few years ago because my mom used to watch her podcasts and still does, and I eventually started listening to her more than my mom!

In January of 2018 when I was 14, I got to meet Mrs. Terri at the Next Conference in Rockwall, Dallas. While speaking during one of the sessions, she made a statement that has stuck with me since then, "*Somebody in need is waiting on the other side of your obedience*" and it stirred me up to start writing. I started writing that evening when we got to the hotel. On our way home, I was writing on the plane. I did not stop writing until I finished the book. I will, therefore, like to say a big thank you to her for stirring me up to write this book and also for writing the foreword for the book. I am so grateful!

I appreciate my dad, David Olabode, and my siblings; Feranmi, Fiyibomi, and Divine. Thank you all for your help during the writing of this book!

My profound gratitude goes to the staff, parents, and students of Cornerstone Christian School, Abbotsford, BC, Canada, who daily prayed for me during those trying years.

I am grateful for the nurses and doctors of the BC Children's Hospital for their patience, love, and care for me during those times when they had to deal with how difficult a patient I was. To my oncologist, Dr. Kirk Schultz, thank you for your excellence in service. To my social worker at the time, Aunty Susara (like we called her), thank you for all your love and care. To all the special groups of volunteers that make the lives of children with terminal illnesses much easier, thank you.

Thank you, Make-A-Wish Foundation for sending my family on an all-expense-paid trip to Disney World, Florida. You are the best.

To the awesome staff and volunteers who serve at Camp Good Times every year to bring joy to families with children suffering from terminal illnesses, thank you!

Lastly, there were so many aunties, uncles, friends, and families that prayed for me during those years I was sick. I am very grateful!

FOREWORD

I want to introduce you to my amazing new friend. His name is Fikayomi Olabode; he is only 17 years and already a man of great faith.

His journey started at age 8 and it wasn't an easy one. Still, it is a testimony of personal victory (overcoming cancer). It will inspire you in your journey to never give up.

His story will touch your hearts as it did mine and encourage your faith no matter your age.

As his dad says, "*God turned a very sick grumpy, bitter, impatient, and complaining boy into a compassionate (healed) and God-loving boy.*"

With a dream in your heart and faith in God, you can do anything. I loved his story and highly recommend his book.

Terri Savelle Foy

Success Coach & Cheerleader of Dreams,

Rockwall, Texas.

INTRODUCTION

This book is probably the best thing that has come out of having cancer.

I am so excited about this book. My aim for writing is for it to be a blessing to you. It is also written to encourage anyone that might be going through a hard time in their lives or need healing in their body.

Robert H. Schuller was known to say, "*Tough times don't last but tough people do*"

In life, we sometimes go through times that seem so dark, you wonder if you will ever find the way out. The truth, though, is that God will always make sure you get out if you trust Him for a solution.

As you read this book, my prayer is that you will be encouraged, strengthened, and motivated to believe God for the impossible. I was told during my days of sickness that I will never be able to play soccer again. I was told that I will not be taller than 5 feet 6 inches, but today, I play soccer daily, I am 5 feet 6 inches tall, and I am on no medication. I am completely healed and whole.

Only God could have done this miracle and He can do it for you too if only you believe.

Sit back and enjoy reading my story of faith.

Fikayomi

TABLE OF CONTENT

PART 1: FIKAYOMI'S PERSPECTIVE

The Pain I Went Through

It all started one day when I was 8 years old. At the time, I began to realize that I was getting tired quickly when I did anything active even when it was for a brief period. It was getting so bad that my mom started to notice. She took me to our family doctor and asked him to do tests on me. He kept saying they couldn't find anything, but because my mom persisted, the doctor did all the tests and even extra tests on me. And then all we could do was wait for the results.

I still remember that evening, like yesterday, when our family doctor called my dad that he needed to see him immediately. He came back with the news of the diagnosis made. It was Acute Lymphatic Leukaemia, also known as ALL or cancer of the blood.

It was such a bitter pill for all of us to swallow. The doctor said my dad and I had to leave for the children's hospital straight away. We waited for the oncologists (An oncologist is a doctor who treats and provides medical care for a person diagnosed with cancer) who were quite busy, but we had our weekly Bible Study at church that evening, so we left for church and then returned to the hospital after the bible study.

We picked a few clothes since we didn't know how long we were going to be gone. My mom and my siblings had to stay back because there was school the next day, but a family friend who was like an aunty to me went with us. When we got to the hospital, there was a whole team of people waiting for us. We stayed the night, and a press conference was scheduled for the next day with my parents. The next day was quite interesting as it wasn't just the oncologists who were there to see my parents. Still, there was a chaplain, a social worker, and not one oncologist, but three.

During the meeting, they explained to my parents what Leukemia was, what it does to the blood and the body. They even said to my parents, "*If we don't treat him, he's going to die.*"

All this while, I was just lying in the hospital room.

Hopes Dashed

Right about then, I realized that I wouldn't be able to play soccer (soccer is what I've always loved to do). I got so upset because I thought being angry was the only way to deal with it. That first year, I missed 133 days of school, and during that time, I dreaded going to school because the days I did go, I couldn't do gym class and couldn't play outside. It just made me so angry. The medications I was taking had such adverse side effects that it just added to the bitterness and anger that I was already feeling like an 8-year-old boy going through such an ordeal.

I wished I had just been playing on a soccer team and enjoying grade 3 like every other 8-year-old boy was doing. If you had met me at that time and met me now, you wouldn't think I'm the same person. I started going through treatment, and I hated it with a capital 'H.' It was so bad when they tried giving me shots back then as I would fight the nurses, scream, and shout at them, but they must have been specially trained because they were so patient.

Now when we go to the hospital every six months for checkups, they jokingly call me "*Fighting David.*" That's because they remembered how I used to fight the nurses during my hospital stays. If you had wanted to give me a shot, you would have had to be ready to fight. At the time, I hated any form of pain, and I used to try getting out of it. When I look back, I thank God for the verse in Romans 8:28. It says,

"*And we know that all things, work together for good to those who love God, to those who are the called; according to his purpose.*"

It taught me that for everything that was happening in my life, God was making something good happen through it.

The First Year Was Hard

During the first year of treatment, I spent a lot of time in the hospital. I spent a lot of time there, it became like a second home to me. The medications I was using made me lose my appetite. I barely ate anything such that I became very skinny.

At the time, I would look at myself in the mirror, and I wouldn't recognize myself. Some nights, I felt like all I could do was lay there on the bed and cry, and I always felt horrible. I felt there was nothing I could do about this and it is so hard to describe how I was living like this every day.

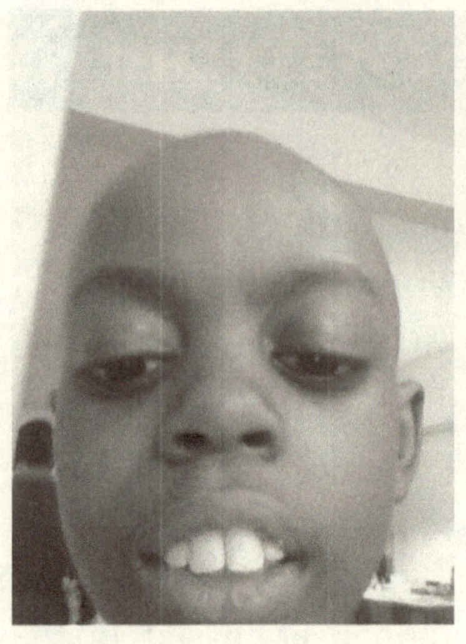

I want to thank God for people that gave us hope like Dr. Charles Stanley. He was the person I remember watching on the TV at the top left corner of the hospital room every Sunday night with my mom as she and my dad would take turns staying with me during this time.

It was a tough time for the whole family, mainly because I had siblings who had to go to school and go about their normal activities. The second reason was that my dad, being a pastor, had to preach during this time even though his son had Leukemia. He had to teach every Sunday so he would stay with me Monday to Friday, and my mom would stay with me Saturday and Sunday and go home on Monday. That was how it worked for about a year.

I had to change the way I slept because I was the type of person who sleeps face down on the pillow. I couldn't do that anymore because they did a surgery to put a thing called a V.A.D. (Ventricular Assist Device) in my chest. It was to provide access to my veins for the delivery of IV (Intravenous) medications and chemotherapy.

This first year was horrible, I couldn't do anything active like play soccer which is my favorite sport. I couldn't go to school (Remember, I missed 133 days of school in the first year), and even on the rare occasions when I did get to go to school, it wasn't fun at all because I couldn't do gym class or go outside at recess. I just didn't have the type of energy the rest of my classmates had. It was so bad that I couldn't even play tag for 5 minutes without losing all my strength. It just made me feel like I was powerless and that I wasn't a regular 8 or 9 years old. I felt it was just so unfair for me to have cancer. I always thought that I didn't deserve to have it, so I would always ask God, "*Why does it have to be me who has cancer? Why can't someone else have it instead of me?*"

That year, I was in the hospital almost all year-round. By this point, I couldn't go to the bathroom by myself. If you had met me at that time, you would be amazed at the person I am now. Before I had cancer, I was a very mean, cruel, and negative person. I would have fit perfectly in the description of a grumpy old man who hates everyone. I am just really grateful to God and my mom (who prayed that I would become a compassionate person) I am now a love being and happy person.

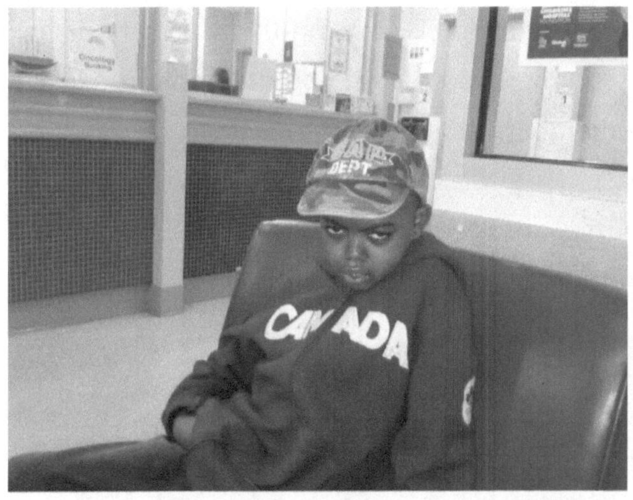

So, as you have read, the first year was a huge struggle for us. Let me tell you something that describes how I felt during the second year.

The Second Year

I have two brothers; Feranmi and Fiyibomi. They used to come and visit me or let me say they were meant to be visiting me, but they were not really visiting me. The hospital had a lot of toys and video game consoles to keep our minds off the sickness or disease we were fighting. So, my brothers, Feranmi and Fiyibomi, loved playing on the Nintendo D.S.'s (remember, they were meant to be visiting me!). One day, they came to visit me. Of course, my brothers had gone to the games room to get the Nintendo D.S.

When Feranmi & Fiyibomi walked in, they said hello to my mom. They didn't even say hello to me. They acted as if I wasn't even there. It made me very sad that my brothers didn't also want to talk or interact with me at all. After they had left, I told my mom in a sad, disappointed, and angry voice, "*I don't want them to come again. They don't ever want to play with me*" Indirectly, I said, "*I don't want to have to bear the pain of them coming and not talking or interacting with me again.*" For me, the hardest year was the second year because of this incident. I felt like everyone had ganged up against me, thrown me into a pit, and left me there. At this point, I started to realize that God was my best friend and that like Deuteronomy 31:6 (ESV) says,

"*He will not leave you or forsake you.*"

And that's exactly how it felt during that particular chapter in my life. I am thankful that God was there for me, comforted me, and was there to shower me the love that I desperately needed at the time. This was because I felt all alone most of the time – like no one else was there for me.

There was a level of love and acceptance that I was used to while growing up. I was used to being accepted and loved by my friends and family. It was just a horrible feeling being known around the school as the boy with cancer. You would think that would have encouraged me; instead, I think it did the opposite.

Another thing that bothered me was when people said they hoped I would get better soon, it made me angrier than I already was. However, I never told anyone that I didn't like them saying that to me. My anger was one big thing I had to learn to start dealing with. I used to get angry quickly, and even after cancer, I still had to deal with it. I had to ask God to help me exercise self-control and not get angry at people because whenever I get mad at people, it usually results in something unpleasant.

When I was in grade 9, I got suspended, and after that, I had to ask myself if I had thoroughly dealt with my anger? And it was almost as soon as I prayed that God revealed to me that dealing with one's anger is like trying to deal with every other type of sin. You have to seek God and run away from it every day, because if you stop one day and say, "*Oh, I think I have gotten away from anger. I think I can stop running*", what will happen is that you will start to see yourself drifting back towards that sin, and soon enough if you don't start running, you will start committing that sin again. You will then wonder, "*I thought I had gotten away from this sin.*" To stop running from sin can be likened to refusing to paddle away from a strong current, soon enough, you will find yourself being pulled into that current.

Every morning, one of my declarations is, "*God, please help me to exhibit the fruits of the Spirit today, everywhere I go, and in everything I do.*" And after I say this every morning, I remember what the Bible says, "*Faith without works (or actions) is dead.*" Or, as I heard my grade 9 teacher say many times to me, "*Talk is cheap*" and I think that quote is accurate. Let me give you an example. If a man said, "*I need to start losing weight*", but never took action, he would just stay fat, wouldn't he? And that's how it works with anything in your life. So, if that fat person starts eating healthy and doing everything it takes to become slim, he will eventually be slim. If you use that method in any area of your life, it works. I'm saying this because I have used this in my life and still do. It indeed works. You can try it out.

God Changed Me from The Inside

I finally started to learn that I had to start dealing with my bad attitude. I slowly started becoming more and more of a kind and compassionate person. It was not easy, and it didn't happen overnight, it was a day to day process which I still practice to date. I still have to go through every day with God helping me day by day, step by step.

Another thing that I struggled with during my time at the hospital, especially the first and second year, was that I could not eat as much as I was used to. I still remember how my mom would bring me food (because I didn't like eating the hospital food) I used to get so excited before she arrived, but as soon as the food was handed over to me, I could only eat a little bit before I felt full. I wanted to eat more, but my tummy could just not take it. I always desired to eat the whole thing, but with all the chemotherapy and medications I was taking, my body just couldn't handle as much food. It bothered me because, on a normal day, I liked eating well. Interestingly, during that time, my favorite food became mashed potatoes (maybe because it was so easy to digest)

I think mashed potatoes are a great example of the type of person I was beginning to become in shape. Before I had cancer, I was like a significant heavyweight on a person's back that you had to carry around. However, I started to become less and less like a featherweight during the time I had cancer. Eventually, I became light and enjoyable, like mashed potatoes. From my perspective, I think that is how God created all people to be.

There Is Power in The Word of God

Many people think that God uses sickness to teach us a lesson, but let me tell you that it is not true! That's like saying, you lost your job because God wants to teach you a lesson! It just doesn't seem to make sense. I know many Christians grow up thinking that when sickness happens, God uses it to teach us a lesson or get something across to us.

If you read the Bible, it says that "*Jesus bore our sicknesses and diseases*" (Isaiah 53:4-5 Paraphrased).

Why do so many people believe this lie? I think a lot of people just don't and haven't seen this in their Bible. Many people see this in their Bible but don't put it into action in their own lives, so when sickness comes, the first thing they do is turn to medicine as they haven't put those healings scriptures in their hearts. To me, what didn't seem so important before I was sick now became so important. The importance of storing the Word of God in one's heart became so real when I was faced with cancer and had to fight it head-on with those scriptures I had stored in my heart.

I say this because I saw that if my parents had not put the Word of God in their hearts before we found out that I had Leukemia, it would have been harder to start storing these scriptures in their hearts. When the doctors said I had cancer, one of the first things my dad said was, *"I rebuke that in the name of Jesus!"*

I remember that so well. Another thing was that my mom and dad always told me that "*I was a child of covenant,*" and that was eventually the way I started to think of myself. It became so real to me that no matter what type of negative report the doctors or nurses brought, I began to say to myself, *"That doesn't affect me. I'm a child of covenant*!"

More Interesting Stories

There was one story I forgot to narrate at the beginning. This happened before I was diagnosed with cancer. One night, while I was watching the TV with my brothers, I went to the kitchen to get some water. I had just finished drinking a glass of water, put the glass down by the sink, and proceeded upstairs to get something from my room. Before I even climbed one of the stairs, all of a sudden, I felt something coming up in my throat. Before I knew it, I threw up red blood clots! (I still remember what I wanted to get from my room!) That was when my mom realized there was something wrong.

Now, let's continue the initial story. Let me tell you about what it felt like taking medicine every day and needles almost every week? In the beginning, all I had was the necessary needles because, at first, when they started trying to give me shots, I would kick, scream, and yell. After all, they were so painful and I hated them (now I love taking shots!) I particularly remember one day when I did my usual kicking, screaming, and yelling. Three people had to hold me down as I yelled. Just when I thought they were done with me, then came the horrible news; they didn't get enough blood from that one spot on my arm, so they had to give me another shot. Being my strong-willed 10-year-old self, I hid under the chairs and locked my hands onto them, and I was determined not to let go of those chairs. I felt it was unfair and shouldn't have to suffer one shot, let alone 2 shots. When I was in grade 6, I had to take 4 shots on the same day! But somehow they got me off the chair. This time, they had 4 people holding me down while I was doing my kicking, screaming, and yelling, but they still gave me the shot, and thankfully, they didn't have to do it again.

Surgeries Are Hard

I remember my first surgery very well. We had to walk to this strange room, and then the surgeons talked among themselves for a bit while I was watching "*Go Diego Go*." When they were about to start the surgery, they gave me a sleeping medicine through the intravenous tube put in my arm, which made me fall asleep.

I simply remember waking up after the surgery to find that they had implanted a device in my chest. It was called a VAD (Ventricular Assist Device). It was to help the medical personnel extract blood quickly from my veins without me screaming and shouting.

The only challenge was that it was very uncomfortable and made sleeping face down almost impossible. Now that I had the VAD in my chest, I couldn't do that. I found it very hard to sleep facing the left or the right. Even now, when I go to bed, I keep tossing and turning before eventually falling asleep.

Having the VAD in my chest was tough because it felt like having a needle in your chest. Whenever I tried to do something active, the VAD will move around, and I will feel like someone was putting a needle in my chest and not taking it out. I still couldn't do anything active, and I was still outraged that I was the person who had to be sick and not someone else.

Hospital Life Was Not Fun

My mom would always tell me a verse from Romans 8:28 that says,

"*And we know that all things work together for good to those who love God, to those who are the called according to his purpose.*"

Hearing that verse almost daily started to help me. I was still angry that I couldn't play soccer, go to school, or do anything active. During that time, I spent a lot of my time playing video games to take my mind away from the sickness. I was fighting every day. I also started making friends with some of the other children who were also fighting life-threatening diseases. We would play with toys and video games to get our minds away from all the stuff we had to deal with.

For a little time, we would feel like children who didn't have life-threatening diseases, and it felt great not having to think about what medications we would have to take later. There was a particular medication that I completely hated, a lot of the time when I took it, I would throw up, and it tasted horrible.

Scary Surgeries

I still had to do chemotherapy and take medications, but it slowly started becoming less and less. Gradually, I did not have to be at the hospital 5 days a week anymore. I started going like 2-3 days a week in the process, I started gaining weight a bit more, and everything was going great. However, there was one more big hurdle to jump over. I had to have my second surgery. I had many thoughts in my head that night. Thoughts like,

"*What if I die during the surgery*?

What if they don't do the surgery right?

What if I wake up during the surgery?

What will happen to my chest?

I was even more scared about this surgery than the first one. But that night, I somehow found a way to go to sleep. The next morning I woke up late, and I found out that I woke up right before the surgery and when I realized they were going to start the operation. I started yelling, asking for my dad. They tried to calm me down, but I didn't calm down until they brought my dad in who talked to me for a short period, and then once I was calm enough, they gave me a shot, and I fell asleep.

While I was sleeping, I felt this peace washing over me, and I saw Jesus' face. He looked so kind and caring, and I remember him telling me, "*Don't be afraid Fikayomi, you're not going to die.*" After that, I remember for a while just seeing pitch black, and then suddenly, I remember someone saying my name as I slowly opened my eyes. I started lifting my head, but when I tried to sit up, my head hurt; everything was blurry. I felt super dizzy, so I laid my head back down on the pillow, and I tried to look up at the clock to see what time it was, but I couldn't see the time, all I could see was the clock spinning in circles. It just made me dizzier and dizzier. I remember everything went black again.

Some Struggles I Faced

I remember that after the second surgery, I took some time to think about everything that had happened to me. While I was thinking about everything, the devil started telling me lies. He said, "*You're not normal*" and "*Your friends won't like you because you had cancer,*" I chose to believe those lies, and it affected me. I still remember, when I would be playing with my friends, the devil would say to me. "*You aren't good enough to be friends with them,*" "*They're just pretending to be your friends because the teacher told everyone to be nice to you.*" It sounded so true, I started believing the lies. It was like that whenever I was in my class or even with my best friends, I felt like I wasn't meant to be friends with them.

Whenever somebody, really anybody in the school, says something to me, I will act like I didn't care about what they were saying to me. The truth, though, was I did care about what they said to me. When I lay in my bed at night, I will be there crying for long. I say to myself over and over, "*Nobody loves me,*" "*Everybody hates me,*" I will then punch myself in the face and whisper to myself, "*What's wrong with you?*" *Why can't you just be normal like everybody else?*" "*Why do you always have to be so stupid and dumb?*"

It didn't help that there was a boy in my class who always called me an idiot, told me that I wasn't good at soccer and that I didn't deserve any friends. For a while, I struggled to be confident in myself, Fikayomi Olabode. I had always struggled with being confident in who I was and didn't know what to do. I told myself, "*You are dumb, stupid, and don't deserve any friends because you're an idiot who had cancer. You're a weirdo.*"

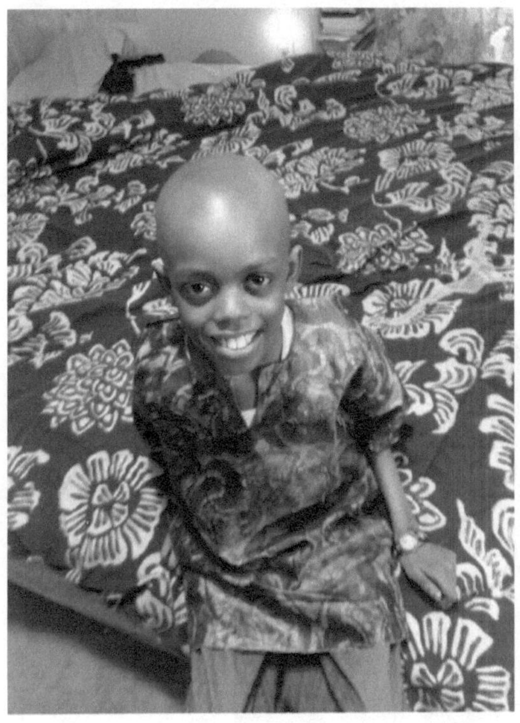

After that incident, I just became more insecure about myself. I never felt like I was good enough just being myself. This was a tough time, but I always tried to remember,

"All things work together for the good of those who love God, who have been called according to his purpose."

Part 2: MY FAMILY'S PERSPECTIVE

Feranmi's Viewpoint (My Younger brother)

I don't remember much of when Fikayomi was sick, but I do remember praying for him almost every day. Fikayomi missed a lot of school time, and I missed him a lot. I was also told I got distracted easily and stared off into space a lot. When we went to the hospital to visit him, I spent more time playing *Mario Bros* than actually talking to him. He was always cranky, and would rather play *Fifa* with Fiyibomi. He still got angry at me anyway.

Fikayomi didn't like the food at the hospital, so we brought him food, even though he only ate a little bit of food, and then he'll say he was full. I also remember crying myself to sleep a few times, wondering if he would die. I was happy, however, when I found out that we were going to Disney World. We barely made it to our flight, and I can still remember Fikayomi just crying. My dad was assuring him that we would make it to the plane, and if we didn't, that he would buy new tickets, and we will still go. We got there, on the last call, and got on the plane.

When we got to Florida, a man held up a sign that had our name on it, and he took us to get our stuff and rent a car. After that, we got directions, and after a few wrong turns and almost one hour of driving, we reached Give Kids The World, where we stayed for eight days. When we got there, it was night, but it was still 20 degrees outside! We had a fantastic time there. We got milkshakes and ice cream any time we wanted. We went to almost every Disney Park and had a badge that let us go to the front of the line for autographs! We were given some money to buy souvenirs with, and we still have some of those souvenirs now.

During that time, my younger brother, Fiyibomi, and sister, Divine, were turning 5 and 2 respectively. They didn't understand what was going on because they were so young. On one of the days, my sister almost caused a car accident by getting out of her car seat, on the highway. My brother, Fiyibomi, did not understand what was going on because he was so young. He just went with us and played video games.

I'm so glad God healed Fikayomi. I'm happy he doesn't have to go through those hard hospital experiences anymore.

My Mom's Viewpoint

The Very Beginning

I'm so grateful to God that I can write about this incident almost 9 years after. It's so funny how time goes by so fast. Looking back, it all seems clear, and I can almost remember everything that happened back then.

Fikayomi was and still is a soccer boy. He had loved the game of soccer from when he about 2 years old. He would play soccer with any object he came across that looked like a ball. He grew up like this until he was eight years old. At that time, I noticed that when I gave him household chores to complete, he will take his time and rest in-between doing the chores. This was very unlike him since he was a very active boy. It got me worried such that I took him to the doctor for a checkup. Our trip to the family doctor did not yield any fruit really as they could not find anything wrong with him. However, I was not satisfied, so I asked for further tests to be done, and thank God for the family doctor that we had, he agreed. He was thorough and ran all tests possible.

During the period when the tests were going on, on one of the days, Fikayomi began to throw up blood clots. It was terrifying such that we had to rush him to the emergency unit. To our amazement, even though we were there for a good number of hours, the doctor told us that he could not find anything wrong with Fikayomi and that we should take him home, which we did. Later, when I related this to my family doctor, he said that the doctor in the emergency unit should not have sent us home because throwing up blood clots was the first sign of Leukemia.

The Story Continues

I still remember vividly, late one afternoon, while getting ready to go for bible studies; our family doctor called my house and asked to speak to my husband. He asked my husband to come and see him right away. My husband went to see him straight away and was told the "News" that the test result was out. It was not good news for us. It revealed that Fikayomi, my son, was diagnosed with **Acute Lymphomic Leukemia** (ALL) - cancer of the blood. He further said that the oncologists were waiting for my husband and son at B.C. Children's Hospital in Vancouver, BC, Canada and that they had to go immediately.

They proceeded to go as soon as the bible study was over, taking a change of clothes.

The Briefing

The next day, I drove with our three other children to the hospital, which was 1 hour away from our house. It was a challenging drive because I did not know what awaited me at the hospital, and all sorts of thoughts went through my mind. When we got to the hospital, my husband mentioned that there was a briefing with the medical team. I assumed that it was just going to be the oncologist and us. I was quite surprised when I walked into the room and saw so many people seated. Three oncologists, a social worker, a chaplain, and I think there was one other medical personnel.

I could not understand why all these people needed to be in the room. It was so scary. After introducing themselves, the Head Oncologist told us that Fikayomi had been diagnosed with Leukemia. He went on to say that if they did not start treatment straight away, my son would die.

That was when all hell broke loose. My husband flared up as soon as he heard those words saying "*My son will not die even if you don't treat him. If my son was not a minor, I know where I would take him, and he would be healed.*" I attempted to calm him down by stepping on his feet, but he went ahead to make his point clear. He hated the fact that they believed that if they did not treat him, he would die. All I said to them was that the same way every product has a manufacturer, my son also had a manufacturer – God. I told them that they should do all they could do scientifically. I will go back to my son's manufacturer, God. He would reset my son back to factory setting like a cell phone is reset back to factory setting when it malfunctions. They looked at my husband, and I like we were nutcases. At the end of the briefing, we authorized them to go ahead with his treatment, and the journey began.

One Day at A Time

From that time on, things changed. The first year was tough because we had three other children and could not put their lives on hold because one of our children was sick. Life still had to go on, it just went on differently. We found a way to devise a schedule to work for us. My husband stayed with him from Monday to Saturday. I then come and swap with him and stay over between Saturday and Monday so that my husband could preach at church on Sunday.

It was a very trying period in our lives. However, it was a time when we learned to lean on God and depend on him alone. Some days while driving to the hospital, I would start crying, asking God when this ordeal would end. At the time, it seemed we could not see the light at the end of the tunnel. During this time, God gave me a scripture, which became my lifeline. It was Philippians 4:6-7,

"*Be careful for nothing; but in everything by prayer and supplication with thanksgiving let your requests be made known unto God. And the peace of God, which passeth all understanding, shall keep your hearts and minds through Christ Jesus*".

These two verses carried us along for the duration of the sickness. Just when it seemed like we were starting to get weary, God gave us another word from Proverbs 24:10

"*If thou faint in the day of adversity, thy strength is small.*" (KJV)

At the time, it was so overwhelming that we could only handle one day at a time. I remember I will ask God to give each of us strength for each day because I knew that was all we needed.

With information from the doctors and nurses, we noticed they shared too much information regarding how long the treatment would be and what it entailed with Fikayomi. We found out that when they tried to tell him too much, he switched off mentally or freaked out because it scared him. We had to warn them to give us the information, and we would relate it to him in *child language*.

The ICU Scare

Towards the end of Fikayomi's treatment, when he was getting ready to start his remission, a terrible event occurred. I was asleep on one of the Saturday nights that I stayed at the hospital, I suddenly woke up praying in the spirit. I sensed all was not well, as I got up, I glanced at the bed of my son to see the vision of an old woman that seemed to have been sent to finish up the business of making sure my son did not survive.

Straightaway, I started praying in tongues because I did not know how else to pray. I kept praying, asking the Holy Ghost to rain fire on her until I felt peace in my spirit. It was about 2 am, and because I knew my husband was going to preach the next morning, I could not call him. I could not go back to sleep, so I kept praying in the spirit. At about 3 am, the doctor came in to check on my son. I asked her if everything was okay, and she said yes and left. At about 4 am, she came back in and checked his heart, now I was getting worried even though she told me that everything was okay. That was somewhat strange because we rarely saw the doctors on weekends unless it was urgent. Between 5 am and 6 am, she was back, saying that he had to be taken downstairs for an x-ray. That was when I knew everything was not okay. This all happened so fast, it seemed like I was watching a movie. From the x-ray room, he was rushed to the ICU (Intensive Care Unit). By this time, he was in a coma, it seemed so strange for a boy that had been perfectly okay the previous day.

I proceeded to call one of our senior pastors and his wife to pray along with us and raise a prayer altar. I sat there in the ICU room declaring that "*My son will not die but live to declare the goodness of the lord.*" It seemed like the darkest time of my life. Later that day, that senior pastor and his wife came to pray with me in the hospital as well as other people, and I just had to hold on in faith, believing God had healed him. When my husband called later in the day asking if everything was okay, I recounted the order of events. He mentioned that the Holy Spirit had woken him up about the same time that night when I saw the vision of the old woman. He said even though he did not know what was going on, he was led to pray in the spirit, and he did until he felt peace in his heart. Before the call ended, he decreed that by the time he got to the hospital the next day, his son would have been out of the coma and back in his room upstairs and it happened as he said.

The VAD (Ventricular Assistance Device), which had been inserted into his chest to aid him in taking shots for blood work had been infected. Just like he had to have surgery to insert it, he had to have another surgery to take it out. They took it out but found out that his heart had been affected, and that was why he ended up in ICU. So, he had to start using medication for his heart and see the cardiologist from time to time in addition to all the other drugs he was already using.

When this incident occurred, my husband and I agreed in prayer that Fikayomi would only use the heart medication for that one year and that God will give him the heart like that of a brand new baby. One year later, it did happen. I will always remember the day my husband came home and showed me the doctor's note stating that Fikayomi did not have to go to the heart clinic anymore. He also mentioned that the cardiologist said that Fikayomi would not have to come back to see them again because his heart was doing well and looked like the heart of a brand new baby. We got the answer to our prayers.

For We Know That All Things Work Together...

Fikayomi did exceptionally well with all his medications. I believe this was so because my husband used to pray over Fikayomi's drugs before he used them, and God was in control of the situation. He would pray that none of the side effects mentioned would happen, and that was exactly what happened. One thing I remember so vividly was that during the sickness, Fikayomi was a very grumpy boy such that I had to start praying that God will bring some good out of this situation. I used Romans 8:28 to encourage Fikayomi a lot.

"*And we know that all things work together for good to them that love God, to them who are the called according to his purpose.*" - KJV

Every time I quoted this verse, he would always say, "*Where is the good, Mummy*? And I will always answer, "*You might not see the good, but if God says all things work together for good then all things will work together for our good*" On one of the days that Fikayomi's oncologist came in, he mentioned an organization called **Make-A-Wish Foundation** and asked if we had heard of it before then. He then told us that it was an organization made up of everyday people who granted a life wish to children diagnosed with terminal illnesses. The form was given to us to fill out, and our doctor signed them and sent them off. The next thing we knew was that the foundation contacted us to interview Fikayomi or David, his middle name, which the hospital staff called him. One of the foundation's representatives came to talk with him at home asking where he would like to visit. He was allowed to choose any destination anywhere in the world. The representative did not know that before Fikayomi fell sick, our children had been asking when we were going to visit Disney World as a family again. The first time we took them, they were young and felt like they had not experienced it. Fikayomi told the representative that he wanted to go to Disney World with the entire family and they immediately started the process. Before the trip, we met the lady that sponsored his trip the weekend before we took the Disney World trip. It allowed us to say thank you to her. Her name was Miss Gabrielle, and she met us at Cactus Club with a big box of goodies for him, and even though he was a bit sick that weekend and also threw up in the restaurant, it was an excellent opportunity to meet her.

The entire trip was great, right from the airport, we were treated like VIP guests as Fikayomi received a badge called a "wish badge," which he had to wear everywhere we went. They called him a "wish child "such that everywhere we went to in the Disney Parks and other entertainment places, the staff took us to the front of the line, and we did not have to line up. It was like a trip to dreamland. Where we stayed was called "Give kids the world." It was a resort where all the wish children could stay while they visited Disney World and other parks. They had events for the children every night, had a 24/7 ice cream parlor, and a 24/7 free food center that you could call whenever you were hungry. They had themed nights, the children got presents every night, and it was a place with everything a child would love to have. It was like Christmas every day.

It was what we needed at the time because we had not realized how tired we had become while going from appointment to appointment, day in, day out. I thank God that he blessed us with this vacation, all expenses paid. They even gave us spending money and a camera went to Fikayomi to take pictures. I can't say thank you enough to BC children's hospital and the wonderful group of people that make up the Make-a-wish Foundation for making so many children happy, especially those children that have to live with various medical conditions for the rest of their lives.

Conclusion

Today, when I look back at how far we have come on this journey, we have so much to give God thanks for. He has indeed been good to us. What started as a trial at the time, God turned into a triumph for us. This experience strengthened our faith, took us deeper in God, helped us know him, and caused us to grow spiritually.

One scenario that I think I would always remember and be grateful to God for happened during Christmas in 2011. Fikayomi had been in the hospital for a couple of days. My husband was not sure if he and Fikayomi would come home for Christmas because his blood counts were low. His siblings and I waited at the edges of our seats, not sure if we were going to spend Christmas with him and their dad. I remember how excited and grateful we were when we heard the horn of the van. It was the best sound ever! It was Christmas Eve and the best Christmas we could ever have gotten. They did not come home empty-handed, the van was full to the brim with toys. The hospital had given them multiple gifts for each of the children. They had so many that we had to give some away. I can go on and on about the "good" that has come out of this seemingly trying time.

I think the biggest thing for me would be how compassionate my son has become. At the start of the treatment, my prayer was that my son will not be bitter but that God will bring some good out of the situation. When I noticed that he was becoming bitter because he had fallen sick, I persisted in my prayers, and God did exceed my expectation regarding bringing good out of the situation. God turned a grumpy, bitter, impatient, and complaining boy into a compassionate, God-loving boy. God made him see life from a new perspective; he saw God redeem his life back from death, from using so many medications to no more drugs, he saw God take him from missing 133 days of school in one year to having perfect attendance in another year. It's been seven years of God's faithfulness and goodness. Thank you, God, for being so kind to us.

My Dad's Viewpoint

The Initial Diagnosis

It all started on August 4th, 2011; the day started as a typical summer day with all the activities planned out. Before this day, Fikayomi's physical appearance had been of great concern to me. He looked pale and somewhat sluggish, which was a sharp contrast to the bubbly eight-year-old soccer-loving boy. Few days before this fateful day, our family doctor had requested another blood work to be done to ascertain what was wrong with Fikayomi after the initial blood work came back inconclusive. Some minutes after 4 pm local time, we received the call from Dr. Chowdhury, our family doctor, instructing us to leave right away for the children's hospital in Vancouver. At about 9 pm, we arrived at the hospital's emergency department. At a few minutes after midnight, the medical staff informed us that Fikayomi needed to undergo further tests the next day.

On August 5th, 2011, my wife came to join me at the hospital, and a team comprising of oncologists, social workers, and other medical professionals informed us that Fikayomi had ALL (a form of a cancer-causing blood disorder). That day was the beginning of a three-and-a-half-year journey where we lived between the hospital and our real family home. The medical professional did not mince words explaining the seriousness of our son's medical condition. The oncologists told us that we would lose Fikayomi if the medical team did not commence treatment immediately. At this point, I lost it because, as a pastor, I have my convictions and faith in divine healing and health. I knew that God would heal my son with or without any medical treatment, but we had to allow him to get the medical care that he needed.

Fikayomi was admitted into the hospital to commence his treatment immediately. They informed us that the first stage of treatment would require him to be in the hospital for the first five to six months. The first surgery he had was for a VAD (Ventricular Assist device) to be inserted in his chest with a tube through his neck region. Through this tube, medications were to be passed into his system to fight the cancerous cells.

The Treatment – Praying over Medications.

The children's hospital became our second home in the first nine months of Fikayomi's treatment. He was allowed to leave the hospital on Christmas Eve in 2011, so we could celebrate Christmas with our family even though his immune system was too low for him to socialize with others or be in a public place freely. During this period, he became very moody and angry, as he didn't understand why the doctors and nurses poked him severally. As a Christian family who believed so much in prayers, we prayed to God, asking for answers to this challenging situation. We got a word from Philippians Chapter 4 verse 6,

"*Be anxious for nothing, but in all things by prayer and supplication, with thanksgiving, make your requests known to God.*"

God used this scripture to encourage us and stir our faith to believe for the seemingly impossible. We got a revelation to pray over every medication before he took them, and so we requested to have the list of all his drugs with their side effects. We would pray over the drugs and ask God to neutralize the side effects. God answered our prayers, as he did not relapse at any of the stages of treatment. As the treatment progressed, he became bloated due to the steroid drugs he used. Fikayomi started losing his hair because of chemotherapy. He lost his weight and his appetite too. He became so thin that you could count his ribs. I remember how he will refuse the food cooked by his mom due to a lack of appetite. It was a very challenging time for all of us. For him, because he spent most of his time being bedridden at the hospital. He also felt like he didn't deserve to be sick when none of his siblings was ill.

He also could not attend school as his immune system was too low, and to avoid contracting infections. He will complain to me about how his siblings will come visiting him and end up playing games in the guest rooms. Just before we could leave the hospital and come for treatments from home, we were exhausted as it had been almost six months of living at the hospital. We got emotionally spent, physically exhausted, and finances were very tight. My wife could not work during this period, and we had to depend on the support from her employer, the Cancer Agency, and friends. Gas cards were given to us to aid our transportation of over two hours to return road trips from Abbotsford to Vancouver in Canada.

Hospital Visits from Home

As the pastor of a growing church, I was stuck in the hospital during the week and only came home on Saturday with the children to attend church service on Sunday. The routine on Monday mornings was to drop the two other boys at their school and drive to Vancouver with my daughter. My absence harmed the church and the Sunday after we came home from the hospital; many of the key leaders and members of the church decided to stay away. It will be fair to say that we came back to an empty church. The process of rebuilding the church and also taking care of our sick child, my three other children, and my wife were of immediate concern to me at this point.

Being home came with a lot of challenges. We had to continually monitor his temperature to make sure he didn't have a fever. On a few occasions, we had to take him to the Emergency Unit of the Abbotsford Regional Hospital. After almost two days of no progress, he was taken by ambulance to the Vancouver Children's Hospital for better professional care. After this stage of on and off visits to the hospital, at a little over one year into the treatment, the whole family started to feel the weight of this situation. The pressure of work (by the way, my wife was working graveyard hours) and caring for the children took its toll on us and we had to dig deep again.

During this period, God gave us another scripture, Proverbs 24:10, "*If you faint in the day of adversity, your strength is small.*" We refused to give up or quit because quitting was not an option! There was a stage of the treatment that we had to spend 3-4 days at the hospital. Fikayomi often had a massive bag of chemo pumped into him, and over the days, he gradually got rid of the fluid until it got to the level that his body weight was required to fight the cancer cells. We did this four times, and we never stayed longer than required. This procedure was another miracle for us. I witnessed many deaths of children (as young as a few months old) at the hospital due to a brain tumor, leukemia, and other forms of cancer.

We were able to use our story to encourage parents whose children were newly diagnosed. We also made many friends. We saw couples get divorced because of the strain caring for a sick child brought on their relationship. Through the thick and thin, God helped us to stay together as a family. We would not have been able to do it without His help. This stage of my story will not be complete without mentioning that my other children felt somehow lost and neglected during this period. We didn't know this until recently when we asked them how they felt when their brother was sick. We did the best we could do during this challenging period of our lives. At the end of the school year, Fikayomi had missed a whopping 133 days of school, and his being sick affected his performance in the next grade, especially in Mathematics and Science.

His school had to put him through an extra class during school hours, and he was also allowed to work on lower grade Mathematics to build his confidence.

A Complication Occurs.

After the first two years of treatment, it became almost a routine until we got to the last stage of treatment before remission. We were looking forward to a reduced visit to the hospital until Fikayomi went for his regular hospital treatment visit and developed some complications. On this fateful Saturday evening, I left the hospital to go home and prepare for the church service the following day being a Sunday. Fikayomi was doing very well, but after my departure, he grew worse, and by late evening and the early hours of the morning, he had to go into the Intensive Care Unit. I didn't know about this until after the church service the next day. When I called my wife to check on them, she narrated what had happened after I left the hospital the previous evening. A strange feeling had also woken me about the same time that night. I wasn't sure why my heart was heavy. I just began to pray in tongues, until I had a release to stop. It was a close shave with death. I assured my wife that my son will be back in his room before I got back to the hospital the next morning, which was a Monday.

After dropping the boys off at their school on Monday, I drove to the hospital in Vancouver in the company my daughter who was four years old at the time. I went straight to the second floor where his room was, as I didn't want to do anything contrary to what I had said the day before, which was that I wanted him out of the ICU before I got to the hospital. I met his social worker, who rightly confirmed that they were cleaning his room before bringing him upstairs. I then proceeded to the ICU, where I met Fikayomi smiling, and he was back to his regular self. Glory be to God! The oncologists discovered that an infection caused the complications through VAD by a virus. The VAD was promptly removed by surgery, but not before Fikayomi's heart had been affected. After this time, he was scheduled to see the heart specialists and had to do echo tests every three months. The cardiologist put Fikayomi on Enalapril, which is a drug to regularize his heart. We kept praying for a miracle that he would no longer have to take the medication and that his heart will be like that of a newborn baby. After taking the drug for about 12 months, we finally got the good news that his heart was made whole. It was like that of a newborn baby, and he didn't have to retake the medication. God answers prayer.

ALL Cleared & The Treats Afterwards.

Fikayomi's journey from being sick to being cancer-free was a roller coaster one. At the end of three and a half years, he was finally in remission. The hospital visit was now every three months, and Fikayomi didn't have to use any more medications and the numerous poking with needles. The head oncologist approached us during one of our numerous visits, and he wanted to know what we did to have such an amazing result with his recovery. It was an opportunity for us to share our faith with him. He agreed that God could do the impossible. It was indeed a victory over the specialists' reports. We also enjoyed some treats during the treatments. Through the Give Kids the World, we were given a seven-nights, eight-day all-expense-paid trip to the Give Kids the World Village in Florida, USA. While in Florida, we got passes to Disney World. Make-A-Wish Foundation also gave us spending money. The children went horse riding; we had too much to eat, drink, and had a chalet to ourselves. It was a memorable experience for everyone.

PART 3: THE "GOOD" THAT CAME OUT OF CANCER

The BC Lions Visit

While I stayed in the hospital, I always dreamed of what it would be like to be a professional athlete and, for example, to win gold in the Olympics or to win the World Cup as a soccer player. In 2011, the BC Lions won the 100th Grey Cup in the CFL (Canadian Football League), and they were bringing the Grey Cup to the BC Children's Hospital. I didn't know that they were coming to the hospital, let alone that they would bring the Grey Cup. It was just a typical cold, December day, and somebody knocked on the door. My dad went to see who it was (I think he already knew), so he opened the door, and before me stood two of the BC lions players who had played in the Grey Cup final, two cheerleaders and the BC Lions mascot, Leo the Lion. My dad and I talked to them for a little bit, and then I took some pictures with them, and I took a picture with Solomon Elimimian, and then they left.

EXIT
88
00
85

RONA
56

I remember I couldn't stop talking about it for days and the best part was I got to lift the Grey Cup. It felt great.

Camp Good Times

Camp Good Times is a camp organized for children who are battling cancer, those in remission, and their families. It is a camp where you get to spend a couple of days unwinding and having fun outdoors. We got to go there in the summer for about four years until we decided to stop going since I was no longer going to the hospital regularly. The Camp was an excellent place. It functioned with a ton of vibrant volunteers. Every family was assigned a chaperone for the children, and they did such a beautiful job. They came to the cabin in the morning to take the children to breakfast, took them to their activities for the day, and were responsible for them while the family was there so the parents could relax. It was always an adventure and fun-filled week.

The first time we went to Camp Good Times, I didn't know what to expect, but my mom and dad told me it would be lots of fun, and it was lots of fun.

There was rock-climbing, hiking, games, canoeing, kayaking, playing in the gym, painting, and many other fun things. There was a year we even got to make wooden cars in the gym, decorate them, and race them against other people.

I think maybe when I'm older, I'll volunteer there for a week or two to serve other people, the same way other people served and helped us.

The Vancouver Canucks Visit

Remember, I mentioned that the Vancouver Canucks players would sometimes visit the BC Children's Hospital in Vancouver.

One day, their mascot came for a Dairy Queen Blizzard party, and I got to meet him and took a few photos with the mascot, Fin the Shark. I could have also met Henrik and Daniel Sedin, but they came on a day I wasn't there!

Fun with Vancouver Whitecaps Players

The Vancouver Whitecaps is one of the three Canadian MLS (Major League Soccer) teams. What happened was that the BC Children's Hospital gave tickets for my whole family to go to a Vancouver Whitecaps game and I was like "Yay!" I had never been to a professional soccer game, but I didn't just get invited to the game, I was one of the children who got to walk onto the pitch with the players in front of the thousands of fans!

Having Fun at A Whitecaps Camp

I couldn't believe we even got to see the players' dressing room, and I got to meet some of the players like Darren Mattocks, Erik Hurtado, Kekua Manneh, and also Camilo Sanvezzo. I was amazed at how kind and caring the players were to us because I, for some reason, thought that they would just walk past us, ignore us, and act like they were big superstars that didn't have to be kind to a group of children they had never met before. But no, they didn't act like that. They didn't even treat us like sick children; they treated us like ordinary children. That's the first thing I noticed about the best athletes in the world, they put themselves in your shoes and ask themselves "*Wouldn't I want a professional soccer player that I love to watch on TV to meet me and be nice to me and treat me like a normal person*?"

I'll never forget the feeling I got when I walked onto that pitch holding the player's hand, looking and hearing thousands of fans cheering. The feeling of looking into the crowd to see my family standing there cheering me on, looking to the bench to see Darren Mattocks wink at me and give me a high five as I walked off the pitch to go watch the guys I had met before the Match play was so elating. See below some pictures of me having fun at a Whitecaps camp

Disney World Trip

I was excited to visit Disney World a second time; I don't remember the first time I went because I was like three years old. A representative of Make-A-Wish foundation (that gives children with illnesses or terminal diseases the opportunity to make a wish for anything) came visiting our house and asked that I make a wish. My first wish was for me to be allowed to make two requests, but the guy said, "*Sorry, we can't do that.*" I was kind of unhappy about it because I wanted to go and see Kaká and also go to Disney World, so I had to choose between Kaká and Disney World. I had to think about it, but I ended up choosing Disney World because I felt like my family needed a break and because it would be fun for everyone, not just me. The Make-A-Wish foundation also gave me a giant gift box, and we even got to go to dinner at the Cactus Club before we traveled. Unfortunately, I threw up at Cactus Club and we had to leave, but everybody was super excited that we were going to Disney World. It was Fiyibomi's first time. He had never been to Disney World, and it was also my little sister's first time. Divine was not even two years old at the time.

The night before our trip, we stayed in this lovely hotel close to the airport because our flight was very early the next morning. We almost could not sleep because we were so excited. When we got to the security checkpoint of Vancouver International Airport, we were hoping to be on time for our flight, only for us to be detained in a particular room for two reasons. The first one was that we were missing a document my little sister was meant to have, and the second was that we had mandarins in our snack bags. My mom had packed them, not knowing that we were not allowed to take fruit through security. The annoying thing was that instead of the security officers to have taken the mandarins from us; they just took us to that room where they explained to us the reason why we were there. I was crying where I sat. We tried to explain to the staff that we were almost late for our flight, but they wouldn't even listen. We were there for a long time, and then the team finally let us leave as we heard the announcer saying, "*The last call for the Olabode family*!" I remember that we all started running with our suitcases and we finally made it! I was so happy when we got on that plane and flew to Disney World.

I must have fallen asleep because the next thing I remember hearing was the Captain saying "*Welcome to Florida Everyone*" I was so happy, I whispered to my brother Feranmi, "*We're in Florida*!" Disney World was amazing, but the best part was that we got to stay at a place called Give-Kids-The-World. My favorite part was that they had a free 24/7 ice cream shop, and you also order food at any time you wanted. I hope I go there again in the future and maybe volunteer at Give kids the world.

The Ice Cream Parlor

The picture with Dr. Seuss

Fun with Mickey

Fun with Blues clues

Fun with Goofy

Horse riding at" Give kids the world."

Fun with Curious George and the man in the yellow hat

I had to be carried around in a stroller in Disneyworld for the long walks because I constantly got tired.

Final Words

I want to say a big thank you for taking the time to read my story. I hope it has encouraged, challenged, strengthened, and motivated you in one way or the other. It was a joy connecting with you.

ABOUT THE AUTHOR

David Fikayomi Olabode is a I7-year-old, fun-loving, soccer boy. He loves God with all of his heart and desires that his story of faith will be a blessing to all who read it.

His greatest desire in life is to play soccer professionally and believes that he is on his way to doing that.

You can connect with him on Instagram - @fikayomiolabode or via email - fikayomiolabode12@gmail.com.

www.ingramcontent.com/pod-product-compliance
Lightning Source LLC
LaVergne TN
LVHW091036150826
845672LV00006BA/1845

* 9 7 9 8 6 8 5 0 5 2 1 5 5 *